Ultimate
Bill and Mail
Organizer

for Busy Professionals

Activinotes

Activinotes

DAILY JOURNALS, PLANNERS, NOTEBOOKS AND OTHER BLANK BOOKS

Copyright 2016

Name: ....

Address: ....

E-mail : ....

Contact no's : ....

....

PAYABLE TRACKER ◀◀◀◀◀◀◀

DATE	BILL	AMOUNT

▶▶▶▶▶▶▶ NOTES

EMAIL TRACKER

DATE	SUBJECT	FROM

REMINDERS

MONDAY

9:00 AM	4:00 PM
10:00 AM	5:00 PM
11:00 AM	6:00 PM
12:00 PM	MUST DOs
1:00 PM	☐
2:00 PM	☐
3:00 PM	☐

TUESDAY

9:00 AM	4:00 PM
10:00 AM	5:00 PM
11:00 AM	6:00 PM
12:00 PM	MUST DOs
1:00 PM	☐
2:00 PM	☐
3:00 PM	☐

WEDNESDAY

9:00 AM	4:00 PM
10:00 AM	5:00 PM
11:00 AM	6:00 PM
12:00 PM	MUST DOs
1:00 PM	☐
2:00 PM	☐
3:00 PM	☐

THURSDAY

9:00 AM	4:00 PM
10:00 AM	5:00 PM
11:00 AM	6:00 PM
12:00 PM	MUST DOs
1:00 PM	☐
2:00 PM	☐
3:00 PM	☐

FRIDAY

9:00 AM	4:00 PM
10:00 AM	5:00 PM
11:00 AM	6:00 PM
12:00 PM	MUST DOs
1:00 PM	☐
2:00 PM	☐
3:00 PM	☐

SATURDAY
APPOINTMENTS

SUNDAY
APPOINTMENTS

MUST DOs
☐
☐

MUST DOs
☐
☐

NOTES

....

....

....

....

MONDAY

9:00 AM	4:00 PM
10:00 AM	5:00 PM
11:00 AM	6:00 PM
12:00 PM	MUST DOs
1:00 PM	☐
2:00 PM	☐
3:00 PM	☐

TUESDAY

9:00 AM	4:00 PM
10:00 AM	5:00 PM
11:00 AM	6:00 PM
12:00 PM	MUST DOs
1:00 PM	☐
2:00 PM	☐
3:00 PM	☐

WEDNESDAY

9:00 AM	4:00 PM
10:00 AM	5:00 PM
11:00 AM	6:00 PM
12:00 PM	MUST DOs
1:00 PM	☐
2:00 PM	☐
3:00 PM	☐

THURSDAY

9:00 AM	4:00 PM
10:00 AM	5:00 PM
11:00 AM	6:00 PM
12:00 PM	MUST DOs
1:00 PM	☐
2:00 PM	☐
3:00 PM	☐

FRIDAY

9:00 AM	4:00 PM
10:00 AM	5:00 PM
11:00 AM	6:00 PM
12:00 PM	MUST DOs
1:00 PM	☐
2:00 PM	☐
3:00 PM	☐

SATURDAY
APPOINTMENTS

SUNDAY
APPOINTMENTS

MUST DOs

☐

☐

MUST DOs

☐

☐

NOTES

....

....

....

....

PAYABLE TRACKER

DATE	BILL	AMOUNT

NOTES

EMAIL TRACKER

DATE	SUBJECT	FROM

REMINDERS

MONDAY

9:00 AM	4:00 PM
10:00 AM	5:00 PM
11:00 AM	6:00 PM
12:00 PM	MUST DOs
1:00 PM	☐
2:00 PM	☐
3:00 PM	☐

TUESDAY

9:00 AM	4:00 PM
10:00 AM	5:00 PM
11:00 AM	6:00 PM
12:00 PM	MUST DOs
1:00 PM	☐
2:00 PM	☐
3:00 PM	☐

WEDNESDAY

9:00 AM	4:00 PM
10:00 AM	5:00 PM
11:00 AM	6:00 PM
12:00 PM	MUST DOs
1:00 PM	☐
2:00 PM	☐
3:00 PM	☐

THURSDAY

9:00 AM	4:00 PM
10:00 AM	5:00 PM
11:00 AM	6:00 PM
12:00 PM	MUST DOs
1:00 PM	☐
2:00 PM	☐
3:00 PM	☐

FRIDAY

9:00 AM	4:00 PM
10:00 AM	5:00 PM
11:00 AM	6:00 PM
12:00 PM	MUST DOs
1:00 PM	☐
2:00 PM	☐
3:00 PM	☐

SATURDAY
APPOINTMENTS

SUNDAY
APPOINTMENTS

MUST DOs
☐
☐

MUST DOs
☐
☐

NOTES

....

....

....

....

MONDAY

9:00 AM	4:00 PM
10:00 AM	5:00 PM
11:00 AM	6:00 PM
12:00 PM	MUST DOs
1:00 PM	☐
2:00 PM	☐
3:00 PM	☐

TUESDAY

9:00 AM	4:00 PM
10:00 AM	5:00 PM
11:00 AM	6:00 PM
12:00 PM	MUST DOs
1:00 PM	☐
2:00 PM	☐
3:00 PM	☐

WEDNESDAY

9:00 AM	4:00 PM
10:00 AM	5:00 PM
11:00 AM	6:00 PM
12:00 PM	MUST DOs
1:00 PM	☐
2:00 PM	☐
3:00 PM	☐

THURSDAY

9:00 AM	4:00 PM
10:00 AM	5:00 PM
11:00 AM	6:00 PM
12:00 PM	MUST DOs
1:00 PM	☐
2:00 PM	☐
3:00 PM	☐

FRIDAY

9:00 AM	4:00 PM
10:00 AM	5:00 PM
11:00 AM	6:00 PM
12:00 PM	MUST DOs
1:00 PM	☐
2:00 PM	☐
3:00 PM	☐

SATURDAY
APPOINTMENTS

SUNDAY
APPOINTMENTS

MUST DOs

☐
☐

MUST DOs

☐
☐

NOTES

....

....

....

....

PAYABLE TRACKER

DATE	BILL	AMOUNT

NOTES

EMAIL TRACKER

DATE	SUBJECT	FROM

REMINDERS

MONDAY

9:00 AM	4:00 PM
10:00 AM	5:00 PM
11:00 AM	6:00 PM
12:00 PM	MUST DOs
1:00 PM	☐
2:00 PM	☐
3:00 PM	☐

TUESDAY

9:00 AM	4:00 PM
10:00 AM	5:00 PM
11:00 AM	6:00 PM
12:00 PM	MUST DOs
1:00 PM	☐
2:00 PM	☐
3:00 PM	☐

WEDNESDAY

9:00 AM	4:00 PM
10:00 AM	5:00 PM
11:00 AM	6:00 PM
12:00 PM	MUST DOs
1:00 PM	☐
2:00 PM	☐
3:00 PM	☐

THURSDAY

9:00 AM	4:00 PM
10:00 AM	5:00 PM
11:00 AM	6:00 PM
12:00 PM	MUST DOs
1:00 PM	☐
2:00 PM	☐
3:00 PM	☐

FRIDAY

9:00 AM	4:00 PM
10:00 AM	5:00 PM
11:00 AM	6:00 PM
12:00 PM	MUST DOs
1:00 PM	☐
2:00 PM	☐
3:00 PM	☐

SATURDAY
APPOINTMENTS

SUNDAY
APPOINTMENTS

MUST DOs

☐

☐

MUST DOs

☐

☐

NOTES

....

....

....

....

MONDAY

9:00 AM	4:00 PM
10:00 AM	5:00 PM
11:00 AM	6:00 PM
12:00 PM	MUST DOs
1:00 PM	☐
2:00 PM	☐
3:00 PM	☐

TUESDAY

9:00 AM	4:00 PM
10:00 AM	5:00 PM
11:00 AM	6:00 PM
12:00 PM	MUST DOs
1:00 PM	☐
2:00 PM	☐
3:00 PM	☐

WEDNESDAY

9:00 AM	4:00 PM
10:00 AM	5:00 PM
11:00 AM	6:00 PM
12:00 PM	MUST DOs
1:00 PM	☐
2:00 PM	☐
3:00 PM	☐

THURSDAY

9:00 AM	4:00 PM
10:00 AM	5:00 PM
11:00 AM	6:00 PM
12:00 PM	MUST DOs
1:00 PM	☐
2:00 PM	☐
3:00 PM	☐

FRIDAY

9:00 AM	4:00 PM
10:00 AM	5:00 PM
11:00 AM	6:00 PM
12:00 PM	MUST DOs
1:00 PM	☐
2:00 PM	☐
3:00 PM	☐

SATURDAY
APPOINTMENTS

SUNDAY
APPOINTMENTS

MUST DOs

☐

☐

MUST DOs

☐

☐

NOTES

....

....

....

....

PAYABLE TRACKER

DATE	BILL	AMOUNT

NOTES

EMAIL TRACKER

DATE	SUBJECT	FROM

REMINDERS

MONDAY

9:00 AM	4:00 PM
10:00 AM	5:00 PM
11:00 AM	6:00 PM
12:00 PM	MUST DOs
1:00 PM	☐
2:00 PM	☐
3:00 PM	☐

TUESDAY

9:00 AM	4:00 PM
10:00 AM	5:00 PM
11:00 AM	6:00 PM
12:00 PM	MUST DOs
1:00 PM	☐
2:00 PM	☐
3:00 PM	☐

WEDNESDAY

9:00 AM	4:00 PM
10:00 AM	5:00 PM
11:00 AM	6:00 PM
12:00 PM	MUST DOs
1:00 PM	☐
2:00 PM	☐
3:00 PM	☐

THURSDAY

9:00 AM	4:00 PM
10:00 AM	5:00 PM
11:00 AM	6:00 PM
12:00 PM	MUST DOs
1:00 PM	☐
2:00 PM	☐
3:00 PM	☐

FRIDAY

9:00 AM	4:00 PM
10:00 AM	5:00 PM
11:00 AM	6:00 PM
12:00 PM	MUST DOs
1:00 PM	☐
2:00 PM	☐
3:00 PM	☐

SATURDAY
APPOINTMENTS

SUNDAY
APPOINTMENTS

MUST DOs
☐
☐

MUST DOs
☐
☐

NOTES

....

....

....

....

MONDAY

9:00 AM	4:00 PM
10:00 AM	5:00 PM
11:00 AM	6:00 PM
12:00 PM	MUST DOs
1:00 PM	☐
2:00 PM	☐
3:00 PM	☐

TUESDAY

9:00 AM	4:00 PM
10:00 AM	5:00 PM
11:00 AM	6:00 PM
12:00 PM	MUST DOs
1:00 PM	☐
2:00 PM	☐
3:00 PM	☐

WEDNESDAY

9:00 AM	4:00 PM
10:00 AM	5:00 PM
11:00 AM	6:00 PM
12:00 PM	MUST DOs
1:00 PM	☐
2:00 PM	☐
3:00 PM	☐

THURSDAY

9:00 AM	4:00 PM
10:00 AM	5:00 PM
11:00 AM	6:00 PM
12:00 PM	MUST DOs
1:00 PM	☐
2:00 PM	☐
3:00 PM	☐

FRIDAY

9:00 AM	4:00 PM
10:00 AM	5:00 PM
11:00 AM	6:00 PM
12:00 PM	MUST DOs
1:00 PM	☐
2:00 PM	☐
3:00 PM	☐

SATURDAY
APPOINTMENTS

SUNDAY
APPOINTMENTS

MUST DOs

☐
☐

MUST DOs

☐
☐

NOTES

....

....

....

....

PAYABLE TRACKER

DATE	BILL	AMOUNT

NOTES

EMAIL TRACKER

DATE	SUBJECT	FROM

REMINDERS

MONDAY

9:00 AM	4:00 PM
10:00 AM	5:00 PM
11:00 AM	6:00 PM
12:00 PM	MUST DOs
1:00 PM	☐
2:00 PM	☐
3:00 PM	☐

TUESDAY

9:00 AM	4:00 PM
10:00 AM	5:00 PM
11:00 AM	6:00 PM
12:00 PM	MUST DOs
1:00 PM	☐
2:00 PM	☐
3:00 PM	☐

WEDNESDAY

9:00 AM	4:00 PM
10:00 AM	5:00 PM
11:00 AM	6:00 PM
12:00 PM	MUST DOs
1:00 PM	☐
2:00 PM	☐
3:00 PM	☐

THURSDAY

9:00 AM	4:00 PM
10:00 AM	5:00 PM
11:00 AM	6:00 PM
12:00 PM	MUST DOs
1:00 PM	☐
2:00 PM	☐
3:00 PM	☐

FRIDAY

9:00 AM	4:00 PM
10:00 AM	5:00 PM
11:00 AM	6:00 PM
12:00 PM	MUST DOs
1:00 PM	☐
2:00 PM	☐
3:00 PM	☐

SATURDAY
APPOINTMENTS

SUNDAY
APPOINTMENTS

MUST DOs
☐
☐

MUST DOs
☐
☐

NOTES
....
....
....
....

MONDAY

9:00 AM	4:00 PM
10:00 AM	5:00 PM
11:00 AM	6:00 PM
12:00 PM	MUST DOs
1:00 PM	☐
2:00 PM	☐
3:00 PM	☐

TUESDAY

9:00 AM	4:00 PM
10:00 AM	5:00 PM
11:00 AM	6:00 PM
12:00 PM	MUST DOs
1:00 PM	☐
2:00 PM	☐
3:00 PM	☐

WEDNESDAY

9:00 AM	4:00 PM
10:00 AM	5:00 PM
11:00 AM	6:00 PM
12:00 PM	MUST DOs
1:00 PM	☐
2:00 PM	☐
3:00 PM	☐

THURSDAY

9:00 AM	4:00 PM
10:00 AM	5:00 PM
11:00 AM	6:00 PM
12:00 PM	MUST DOs
1:00 PM	☐
2:00 PM	☐
3:00 PM	☐

FRIDAY

9:00 AM	4:00 PM
10:00 AM	5:00 PM
11:00 AM	6:00 PM
12:00 PM	MUST DOs
1:00 PM	☐
2:00 PM	☐
3:00 PM	☐

SATURDAY
APPOINTMENTS

SUNDAY
APPOINTMENTS

MUST DOs

☐

☐

MUST DOs

☐

☐

NOTES

PAYABLE TRACKER

DATE	BILL	AMOUNT

NOTES

EMAIL TRACKER

DATE	SUBJECT	FROM

REMINDERS

MONDAY

9:00 AM	4:00 PM
10:00 AM	5:00 PM
11:00 AM	6:00 PM
12:00 PM	MUST DOs
1:00 PM	☐
2:00 PM	☐
3:00 PM	☐

TUESDAY

9:00 AM	4:00 PM
10:00 AM	5:00 PM
11:00 AM	6:00 PM
12:00 PM	MUST DOs
1:00 PM	☐
2:00 PM	☐
3:00 PM	☐

WEDNESDAY

9:00 AM	4:00 PM
10:00 AM	5:00 PM
11:00 AM	6:00 PM
12:00 PM	MUST DOs
1:00 PM	☐
2:00 PM	☐
3:00 PM	☐

THURSDAY

9:00 AM	4:00 PM
10:00 AM	5:00 PM
11:00 AM	6:00 PM
12:00 PM	MUST DOs
1:00 PM	☐
2:00 PM	☐
3:00 PM	☐

FRIDAY

9:00 AM	4:00 PM
10:00 AM	5:00 PM
11:00 AM	6:00 PM
12:00 PM	MUST DOs
1:00 PM	☐
2:00 PM	☐
3:00 PM	☐

SATURDAY
APPOINTMENTS

SUNDAY
APPOINTMENTS

_____

_____

_____

MUST DOs

☐ _____

☐ _____

MUST DOs

☐ _____

☐ _____

NOTES

....

....

....

....

MONDAY

9:00 AM	4:00 PM
10:00 AM	5:00 PM
11:00 AM	6:00 PM
12:00 PM	MUST DOs
1:00 PM	☐
2:00 PM	☐
3:00 PM	☐

TUESDAY

9:00 AM	4:00 PM
10:00 AM	5:00 PM
11:00 AM	6:00 PM
12:00 PM	MUST DOs
1:00 PM	☐
2:00 PM	☐
3:00 PM	☐

WEDNESDAY

9:00 AM	4:00 PM
10:00 AM	5:00 PM
11:00 AM	6:00 PM
12:00 PM	MUST DOs
1:00 PM	☐
2:00 PM	☐
3:00 PM	☐

THURSDAY

9:00 AM	4:00 PM
10:00 AM	5:00 PM
11:00 AM	6:00 PM
12:00 PM	MUST DOs
1:00 PM	☐
2:00 PM	☐
3:00 PM	☐

FRIDAY

9:00 AM	4:00 PM
10:00 AM	5:00 PM
11:00 AM	6:00 PM
12:00 PM	MUST DOs
1:00 PM	☐
2:00 PM	☐
3:00 PM	☐

SATURDAY
APPOINTMENTS

SUNDAY
APPOINTMENTS

MUST DOs

☐
☐

MUST DOs

☐
☐

NOTES

....

....

....

....

PAYABLE TRACKER

DATE	BILL	AMOUNT

NOTES

EMAIL TRACKER

DATE	SUBJECT	FROM

REMINDERS

MONDAY

9:00 AM	4:00 PM
10:00 AM	5:00 PM
11:00 AM	6:00 PM
12:00 PM	MUST DOs
1:00 PM	☐
2:00 PM	☐
3:00 PM	☐

TUESDAY

9:00 AM	4:00 PM
10:00 AM	5:00 PM
11:00 AM	6:00 PM
12:00 PM	MUST DOs
1:00 PM	☐
2:00 PM	☐
3:00 PM	☐

WEDNESDAY

9:00 AM	4:00 PM
10:00 AM	5:00 PM
11:00 AM	6:00 PM
12:00 PM	MUST DOs
1:00 PM	☐
2:00 PM	☐
3:00 PM	☐

THURSDAY

9:00 AM	4:00 PM
10:00 AM	5:00 PM
11:00 AM	6:00 PM
12:00 PM	MUST DOs
1:00 PM	☐
2:00 PM	☐
3:00 PM	☐

FRIDAY

9:00 AM	4:00 PM
10:00 AM	5:00 PM
11:00 AM	6:00 PM
12:00 PM	MUST DOs
1:00 PM	☐
2:00 PM	☐
3:00 PM	☐

SATURDAY
APPOINTMENTS

MUST DOs
☐
☐

SUNDAY
APPOINTMENTS

MUST DOs
☐
☐

NOTES

....

....

....

....

MONDAY

9:00 AM	4:00 PM
10:00 AM	5:00 PM
11:00 AM	6:00 PM
12:00 PM	MUST DOs
1:00 PM	☐
2:00 PM	☐
3:00 PM	☐

TUESDAY

9:00 AM	4:00 PM
10:00 AM	5:00 PM
11:00 AM	6:00 PM
12:00 PM	MUST DOs
1:00 PM	☐
2:00 PM	☐
3:00 PM	☐

WEDNESDAY

9:00 AM	4:00 PM
10:00 AM	5:00 PM
11:00 AM	6:00 PM
12:00 PM	MUST DOs
1:00 PM	☐
2:00 PM	☐
3:00 PM	☐

THURSDAY

9:00 AM	4:00 PM
10:00 AM	5:00 PM
11:00 AM	6:00 PM
12:00 PM	MUST DOs
1:00 PM	☐
2:00 PM	☐
3:00 PM	☐

FRIDAY

9:00 AM	4:00 PM
10:00 AM	5:00 PM
11:00 AM	6:00 PM
12:00 PM	MUST DOs
1:00 PM	☐
2:00 PM	☐
3:00 PM	☐

SATURDAY
APPOINTMENTS

SUNDAY
APPOINTMENTS

MUST DOs

☐

☐

MUST DOs

☐

☐

NOTES

....

....

....

....

PAYABLE TRACKER

DATE	BILL	AMOUNT

NOTES

EMAIL TRACKER

DATE	SUBJECT	FROM

REMINDERS

MONDAY

9:00 AM	4:00 PM
10:00 AM	5:00 PM
11:00 AM	6:00 PM
12:00 PM	MUST DOs
1:00 PM	☐
2:00 PM	☐
3:00 PM	☐

TUESDAY

9:00 AM	4:00 PM
10:00 AM	5:00 PM
11:00 AM	6:00 PM
12:00 PM	MUST DOs
1:00 PM	☐
2:00 PM	☐
3:00 PM	☐

WEDNESDAY

9:00 AM	4:00 PM
10:00 AM	5:00 PM
11:00 AM	6:00 PM
12:00 PM	MUST DOs
1:00 PM	☐
2:00 PM	☐
3:00 PM	☐

THURSDAY

9:00 AM	4:00 PM
10:00 AM	5:00 PM
11:00 AM	6:00 PM
12:00 PM	MUST DOs
1:00 PM	☐
2:00 PM	☐
3:00 PM	☐

FRIDAY

9:00 AM	4:00 PM
10:00 AM	5:00 PM
11:00 AM	6:00 PM
12:00 PM	MUST DOs
1:00 PM	☐
2:00 PM	☐
3:00 PM	☐

SATURDAY
APPOINTMENTS

SUNDAY
APPOINTMENTS

MUST DOs
☐
☐

MUST DOs
☐
☐

NOTES

....

....

....

....

MONDAY

9:00 AM	4:00 PM
10:00 AM	5:00 PM
11:00 AM	6:00 PM
12:00 PM	MUST DOs
1:00 PM	☐
2:00 PM	☐
3:00 PM	☐

TUESDAY

9:00 AM	4:00 PM
10:00 AM	5:00 PM
11:00 AM	6:00 PM
12:00 PM	MUST DOs
1:00 PM	☐
2:00 PM	☐
3:00 PM	☐

WEDNESDAY

9:00 AM	4:00 PM
10:00 AM	5:00 PM
11:00 AM	6:00 PM
12:00 PM	MUST DOs
1:00 PM	☐
2:00 PM	☐
3:00 PM	☐

THURSDAY

9:00 AM	4:00 PM
10:00 AM	5:00 PM
11:00 AM	6:00 PM
12:00 PM	MUST DOs
1:00 PM	☐
2:00 PM	☐
3:00 PM	☐

FRIDAY

9:00 AM	4:00 PM
10:00 AM	5:00 PM
11:00 AM	6:00 PM
12:00 PM	MUST DOs
1:00 PM	☐
2:00 PM	☐
3:00 PM	☐

SATURDAY
APPOINTMENTS

SUNDAY
APPOINTMENTS

MUST DOs

☐

☐

MUST DOs

☐

☐

NOTES

....

....

....

....

PAYABLE TRACKER

DATE	BILL	AMOUNT

NOTES

EMAIL TRACKER

DATE	SUBJECT	FROM

REMINDERS

MONDAY

9:00 AM	4:00 PM
10:00 AM	5:00 PM
11:00 AM	6:00 PM
12:00 PM	MUST DOs
1:00 PM	☐
2:00 PM	☐
3:00 PM	☐

TUESDAY

9:00 AM	4:00 PM
10:00 AM	5:00 PM
11:00 AM	6:00 PM
12:00 PM	MUST DOs
1:00 PM	☐
2:00 PM	☐
3:00 PM	☐

WEDNESDAY

9:00 AM	4:00 PM
10:00 AM	5:00 PM
11:00 AM	6:00 PM
12:00 PM	MUST DOs
1:00 PM	☐
2:00 PM	☐
3:00 PM	☐

THURSDAY

9:00 AM	4:00 PM
10:00 AM	5:00 PM
11:00 AM	6:00 PM
12:00 PM	MUST DOs
1:00 PM	☐
2:00 PM	☐
3:00 PM	☐

FRIDAY

9:00 AM	4:00 PM
10:00 AM	5:00 PM
11:00 AM	6:00 PM
12:00 PM	MUST DOs
1:00 PM	☐
2:00 PM	☐
3:00 PM	☐

SATURDAY
APPOINTMENTS

SUNDAY
APPOINTMENTS

MUST DOs
☐
☐

MUST DOs
☐
☐

NOTES

....

....

....

....

MONDAY

9:00 AM	4:00 PM
10:00 AM	5:00 PM
11:00 AM	6:00 PM
12:00 PM	MUST DOs
1:00 PM	☐
2:00 PM	☐
3:00 PM	☐

TUESDAY

9:00 AM	4:00 PM
10:00 AM	5:00 PM
11:00 AM	6:00 PM
12:00 PM	MUST DOs
1:00 PM	☐
2:00 PM	☐
3:00 PM	☐

WEDNESDAY

9:00 AM	4:00 PM
10:00 AM	5:00 PM
11:00 AM	6:00 PM
12:00 PM	MUST DOs
1:00 PM	☐
2:00 PM	☐
3:00 PM	☐

THURSDAY

9:00 AM	4:00 PM
10:00 AM	5:00 PM
11:00 AM	6:00 PM
12:00 PM	MUST DOs
1:00 PM	☐
2:00 PM	☐
3:00 PM	☐

FRIDAY

9:00 AM	4:00 PM
10:00 AM	5:00 PM
11:00 AM	6:00 PM
12:00 PM	MUST DOs
1:00 PM	☐
2:00 PM	☐
3:00 PM	☐

SATURDAY
APPOINTMENTS

SUNDAY
APPOINTMENTS

MUST DOs
☐
☐

MUST DOs
☐
☐

NOTES

....

....

....

....

PAYABLE TRACKER

DATE	BILL	AMOUNT

NOTES

EMAIL TRACKER

DATE	SUBJECT	FROM

REMINDERS

MONDAY

9:00 AM	4:00 PM
10:00 AM	5:00 PM
11:00 AM	6:00 PM
12:00 PM	MUST DOs
1:00 PM	☐
2:00 PM	☐
3:00 PM	☐

TUESDAY

9:00 AM	4:00 PM
10:00 AM	5:00 PM
11:00 AM	6:00 PM
12:00 PM	MUST DOs
1:00 PM	☐
2:00 PM	☐
3:00 PM	☐

WEDNESDAY

9:00 AM	4:00 PM
10:00 AM	5:00 PM
11:00 AM	6:00 PM
12:00 PM	MUST DOs
1:00 PM	☐
2:00 PM	☐
3:00 PM	☐

THURSDAY

9:00 AM	4:00 PM
10:00 AM	5:00 PM
11:00 AM	6:00 PM
12:00 PM	MUST DOs
1:00 PM	☐
2:00 PM	☐
3:00 PM	☐

FRIDAY

9:00 AM	4:00 PM
10:00 AM	5:00 PM
11:00 AM	6:00 PM
12:00 PM	MUST DOs
1:00 PM	☐
2:00 PM	☐
3:00 PM	☐

SATURDAY
APPOINTMENTS

_____

_____

_____

MUST DOs
☐
☐

SUNDAY
APPOINTMENTS

_____

_____

_____

MUST DOs
☐
☐

NOTES

....

....

....

....

MONDAY

9:00 AM	4:00 PM
10:00 AM	5:00 PM
11:00 AM	6:00 PM
12:00 PM	MUST DOs
1:00 PM	☐
2:00 PM	☐
3:00 PM	☐

TUESDAY

9:00 AM	4:00 PM
10:00 AM	5:00 PM
11:00 AM	6:00 PM
12:00 PM	MUST DOs
1:00 PM	☐
2:00 PM	☐
3:00 PM	☐

WEDNESDAY

9:00 AM	4:00 PM
10:00 AM	5:00 PM
11:00 AM	6:00 PM
12:00 PM	MUST DOs
1:00 PM	☐
2:00 PM	☐
3:00 PM	☐

THURSDAY

9:00 AM	4:00 PM
10:00 AM	5:00 PM
11:00 AM	6:00 PM
12:00 PM	MUST DOs
1:00 PM	☐
2:00 PM	☐
3:00 PM	☐

FRIDAY

9:00 AM	4:00 PM
10:00 AM	5:00 PM
11:00 AM	6:00 PM
12:00 PM	MUST DOs
1:00 PM	☐
2:00 PM	☐
3:00 PM	☐

SATURDAY
APPOINTMENTS

SUNDAY
APPOINTMENTS

MUST DOs
☐
☐

MUST DOs
☐
☐

NOTES

....

....

....

....

PAYABLE TRACKER 《《《《《《《《《《

DATE	BILL	AMOUNT

》》》》》》》》》》 NOTES

_____
_____
_____
_____
_____
_____
_____
_____
_____
_____

EMAIL TRACKER

DATE	SUBJECT	FROM

REMINDERS

MONDAY

9:00 AM	4:00 PM
10:00 AM	5:00 PM
11:00 AM	6:00 PM
12:00 PM	MUST DOs
1:00 PM	☐
2:00 PM	☐
3:00 PM	☐

TUESDAY

9:00 AM	4:00 PM
10:00 AM	5:00 PM
11:00 AM	6:00 PM
12:00 PM	MUST DOs
1:00 PM	☐
2:00 PM	☐
3:00 PM	☐

WEDNESDAY

9:00 AM	4:00 PM
10:00 AM	5:00 PM
11:00 AM	6:00 PM
12:00 PM	MUST DOs
1:00 PM	☐
2:00 PM	☐
3:00 PM	☐

THURSDAY

9:00 AM	4:00 PM
10:00 AM	5:00 PM
11:00 AM	6:00 PM
12:00 PM	MUST DOs
1:00 PM	☐
2:00 PM	☐
3:00 PM	☐

FRIDAY

9:00 AM	4:00 PM
10:00 AM	5:00 PM
11:00 AM	6:00 PM
12:00 PM	MUST DOs
1:00 PM	☐
2:00 PM	☐
3:00 PM	☐

SATURDAY
APPOINTMENTS

SUNDAY
APPOINTMENTS

MUST DOs
☐
☐

MUST DOs
☐
☐

NOTES

....

....

....

....

MONDAY

9:00 AM	4:00 PM
10:00 AM	5:00 PM
11:00 AM	6:00 PM
12:00 PM	MUST DOs
1:00 PM	☐
2:00 PM	☐
3:00 PM	☐

TUESDAY

9:00 AM	4:00 PM
10:00 AM	5:00 PM
11:00 AM	6:00 PM
12:00 PM	MUST DOs
1:00 PM	☐
2:00 PM	☐
3:00 PM	☐

WEDNESDAY

9:00 AM	4:00 PM
10:00 AM	5:00 PM
11:00 AM	6:00 PM
12:00 PM	MUST DOs
1:00 PM	☐
2:00 PM	☐
3:00 PM	☐

THURSDAY

9:00 AM	4:00 PM
10:00 AM	5:00 PM
11:00 AM	6:00 PM
12:00 PM	MUST DOs
1:00 PM	☐
2:00 PM	☐
3:00 PM	☐

FRIDAY

9:00 AM	4:00 PM
10:00 AM	5:00 PM
11:00 AM	6:00 PM
12:00 PM	MUST DOs
1:00 PM	☐
2:00 PM	☐
3:00 PM	☐

SATURDAY
APPOINTMENTS

SUNDAY
APPOINTMENTS

MUST DOs
☐
☐

MUST DOs
☐
☐

NOTES

....

....

....

....

PAYABLE TRACKER

DATE	BILL	AMOUNT

NOTES

EMAIL TRACKER

DATE	SUBJECT	FROM

REMINDERS

MONDAY

9:00 AM	4:00 PM
10:00 AM	5:00 PM
11:00 AM	6:00 PM
12:00 PM	MUST DOs
1:00 PM	☐
2:00 PM	☐
3:00 PM	☐

TUESDAY

9:00 AM	4:00 PM
10:00 AM	5:00 PM
11:00 AM	6:00 PM
12:00 PM	MUST DOs
1:00 PM	☐
2:00 PM	☐
3:00 PM	☐

WEDNESDAY

9:00 AM	4:00 PM
10:00 AM	5:00 PM
11:00 AM	6:00 PM
12:00 PM	MUST DOs
1:00 PM	☐
2:00 PM	☐
3:00 PM	☐

THURSDAY

9:00 AM	4:00 PM
10:00 AM	5:00 PM
11:00 AM	6:00 PM
12:00 PM	MUST DOs
1:00 PM	☐
2:00 PM	☐
3:00 PM	☐

FRIDAY

9:00 AM	4:00 PM
10:00 AM	5:00 PM
11:00 AM	6:00 PM
12:00 PM	MUST DOs
1:00 PM	☐
2:00 PM	☐
3:00 PM	☐

SATURDAY
APPOINTMENTS

SUNDAY
APPOINTMENTS

MUST DOs
☐
☐

MUST DOs
☐
☐

NOTES

....

....

....

....

MONDAY

9:00 AM	4:00 PM
10:00 AM	5:00 PM
11:00 AM	6:00 PM
12:00 PM	MUST DOs
1:00 PM	☐
2:00 PM	☐
3:00 PM	☐

TUESDAY

9:00 AM	4:00 PM
10:00 AM	5:00 PM
11:00 AM	6:00 PM
12:00 PM	MUST DOs
1:00 PM	☐
2:00 PM	☐
3:00 PM	☐

WEDNESDAY

9:00 AM	4:00 PM
10:00 AM	5:00 PM
11:00 AM	6:00 PM
12:00 PM	MUST DOs
1:00 PM	☐
2:00 PM	☐
3:00 PM	☐

THURSDAY

9:00 AM	4:00 PM
10:00 AM	5:00 PM
11:00 AM	6:00 PM
12:00 PM	MUST DOs
1:00 PM	☐
2:00 PM	☐
3:00 PM	☐

FRIDAY

9:00 AM	4:00 PM
10:00 AM	5:00 PM
11:00 AM	6:00 PM
12:00 PM	MUST DOs
1:00 PM	☐
2:00 PM	☐
3:00 PM	☐

SATURDAY
APPOINTMENTS

SUNDAY
APPOINTMENTS

MUST DOs
☐
☐

MUST DOs
☐
☐

NOTES

....

....

....

....

PAYABLE TRACKER

DATE	BILL	AMOUNT

NOTES

_____

_____

_____

_____

_____

_____

_____

_____

_____

EMAIL TRACKER

DATE	SUBJECT	FROM

REMINDERS

MONDAY

9:00 AM	4:00 PM
10:00 AM	5:00 PM
11:00 AM	6:00 PM
12:00 PM	MUST DOs
1:00 PM	☐
2:00 PM	☐
3:00 PM	☐

TUESDAY

9:00 AM	4:00 PM
10:00 AM	5:00 PM
11:00 AM	6:00 PM
12:00 PM	MUST DOs
1:00 PM	☐
2:00 PM	☐
3:00 PM	☐

WEDNESDAY

9:00 AM	4:00 PM
10:00 AM	5:00 PM
11:00 AM	6:00 PM
12:00 PM	MUST DOs
1:00 PM	☐
2:00 PM	☐
3:00 PM	☐

THURSDAY

9:00 AM	4:00 PM
10:00 AM	5:00 PM
11:00 AM	6:00 PM
12:00 PM	MUST DOs
1:00 PM	☐
2:00 PM	☐
3:00 PM	☐

FRIDAY

9:00 AM	4:00 PM
10:00 AM	5:00 PM
11:00 AM	6:00 PM
12:00 PM	MUST DOs
1:00 PM	☐
2:00 PM	☐
3:00 PM	☐

SATURDAY
APPOINTMENTS

SUNDAY
APPOINTMENTS

MUST DOs
☐
☐

MUST DOs
☐
☐

NOTES

MONDAY

9:00 AM	4:00 PM
10:00 AM	5:00 PM
11:00 AM	6:00 PM
12:00 PM	MUST DOs
1:00 PM	☐
2:00 PM	☐
3:00 PM	☐

TUESDAY

9:00 AM	4:00 PM
10:00 AM	5:00 PM
11:00 AM	6:00 PM
12:00 PM	MUST DOs
1:00 PM	☐
2:00 PM	☐
3:00 PM	☐

WEDNESDAY

9:00 AM	4:00 PM
10:00 AM	5:00 PM
11:00 AM	6:00 PM
12:00 PM	MUST DOs
1:00 PM	☐
2:00 PM	☐
3:00 PM	☐

THURSDAY

9:00 AM	4:00 PM
10:00 AM	5:00 PM
11:00 AM	6:00 PM
12:00 PM	MUST DOs
1:00 PM	☐
2:00 PM	☐
3:00 PM	☐

FRIDAY

9:00 AM	4:00 PM
10:00 AM	5:00 PM
11:00 AM	6:00 PM
12:00 PM	MUST DOs
1:00 PM	☐
2:00 PM	☐
3:00 PM	☐

SATURDAY
APPOINTMENTS

SUNDAY
APPOINTMENTS

MUST DOs

☐

☐

MUST DOs

☐

☐

NOTES

....

....

....

....

PAYABLE TRACKER

DATE	BILL	AMOUNT

NOTES

EMAIL TRACKER

DATE	SUBJECT	FROM

REMINDERS

MONDAY

9:00 AM	4:00 PM
10:00 AM	5:00 PM
11:00 AM	6:00 PM
12:00 PM	MUST DOs
1:00 PM	☐
2:00 PM	☐
3:00 PM	☐

TUESDAY

9:00 AM	4:00 PM
10:00 AM	5:00 PM
11:00 AM	6:00 PM
12:00 PM	MUST DOs
1:00 PM	☐
2:00 PM	☐
3:00 PM	☐

WEDNESDAY

9:00 AM	4:00 PM
10:00 AM	5:00 PM
11:00 AM	6:00 PM
12:00 PM	MUST DOs
1:00 PM	☐
2:00 PM	☐
3:00 PM	☐

THURSDAY

9:00 AM	4:00 PM
10:00 AM	5:00 PM
11:00 AM	6:00 PM
12:00 PM	MUST DOs
1:00 PM	☐
2:00 PM	☐
3:00 PM	☐

FRIDAY

9:00 AM	4:00 PM
10:00 AM	5:00 PM
11:00 AM	6:00 PM
12:00 PM	MUST DOs
1:00 PM	☐
2:00 PM	☐
3:00 PM	☐

SATURDAY
APPOINTMENTS

SUNDAY
APPOINTMENTS

MUST DOs
☐
☐

MUST DOs
☐
☐

NOTES

MONDAY

9:00 AM	4:00 PM
10:00 AM	5:00 PM
11:00 AM	6:00 PM
12:00 PM	MUST DOs
1:00 PM	☐
2:00 PM	☐
3:00 PM	☐

TUESDAY

9:00 AM	4:00 PM
10:00 AM	5:00 PM
11:00 AM	6:00 PM
12:00 PM	MUST DOs
1:00 PM	☐
2:00 PM	☐
3:00 PM	☐

WEDNESDAY

9:00 AM	4:00 PM
10:00 AM	5:00 PM
11:00 AM	6:00 PM
12:00 PM	MUST DOs
1:00 PM	☐
2:00 PM	☐
3:00 PM	☐

THURSDAY

9:00 AM	4:00 PM
10:00 AM	5:00 PM
11:00 AM	6:00 PM
12:00 PM	MUST DOs
1:00 PM	☐
2:00 PM	☐
3:00 PM	☐

FRIDAY

9:00 AM	4:00 PM
10:00 AM	5:00 PM
11:00 AM	6:00 PM
12:00 PM	MUST DOs
1:00 PM	☐
2:00 PM	☐
3:00 PM	☐

SATURDAY
APPOINTMENTS

_____

_____

_____

MUST DOs

☐ _____

☐ _____

SUNDAY
APPOINTMENTS

_____

_____

_____

MUST DOs

☐ _____

☐ _____

NOTES

....

....

....

....

PAYABLE TRACKER

DATE	BILL	AMOUNT

NOTES

EMAIL TRACKER

DATE	SUBJECT	FROM

REMINDERS

MONDAY

9:00 AM	4:00 PM
10:00 AM	5:00 PM
11:00 AM	6:00 PM
12:00 PM	MUST DOs
1:00 PM	☐
2:00 PM	☐
3:00 PM	☐

TUESDAY

9:00 AM	4:00 PM
10:00 AM	5:00 PM
11:00 AM	6:00 PM
12:00 PM	MUST DOs
1:00 PM	☐
2:00 PM	☐
3:00 PM	☐

WEDNESDAY

9:00 AM	4:00 PM
10:00 AM	5:00 PM
11:00 AM	6:00 PM
12:00 PM	MUST DOs
1:00 PM	☐
2:00 PM	☐
3:00 PM	☐

THURSDAY

9:00 AM	4:00 PM
10:00 AM	5:00 PM
11:00 AM	6:00 PM
12:00 PM	MUST DOs
1:00 PM	☐
2:00 PM	☐
3:00 PM	☐

FRIDAY

9:00 AM	4:00 PM
10:00 AM	5:00 PM
11:00 AM	6:00 PM
12:00 PM	MUST DOs
1:00 PM	☐
2:00 PM	☐
3:00 PM	☐

SATURDAY
APPOINTMENTS

SUNDAY
APPOINTMENTS

MUST DOs

☐

☐

MUST DOs

☐

☐

NOTES

....

....

....

....

MONDAY

9:00 AM	4:00 PM
10:00 AM	5:00 PM
11:00 AM	6:00 PM
12:00 PM	MUST DOs
1:00 PM	☐
2:00 PM	☐
3:00 PM	☐

TUESDAY

9:00 AM	4:00 PM
10:00 AM	5:00 PM
11:00 AM	6:00 PM
12:00 PM	MUST DOs
1:00 PM	☐
2:00 PM	☐
3:00 PM	☐

WEDNESDAY

9:00 AM	4:00 PM
10:00 AM	5:00 PM
11:00 AM	6:00 PM
12:00 PM	MUST DOs
1:00 PM	☐
2:00 PM	☐
3:00 PM	☐

THURSDAY

9:00 AM	4:00 PM
10:00 AM	5:00 PM
11:00 AM	6:00 PM
12:00 PM	MUST DOs
1:00 PM	☐
2:00 PM	☐
3:00 PM	☐

FRIDAY

9:00 AM	4:00 PM
10:00 AM	5:00 PM
11:00 AM	6:00 PM
12:00 PM	MUST DOs
1:00 PM	☐
2:00 PM	☐
3:00 PM	☐

SATURDAY
APPOINTMENTS

SUNDAY
APPOINTMENTS

MUST DOs

☐
☐

MUST DOs

☐
☐

NOTES

....

....

....

....

PAYABLE TRACKER

DATE	BILL	AMOUNT

NOTES

_____

_____

_____

_____

_____

_____

_____

_____

EMAIL TRACKER

DATE	SUBJECT	FROM

REMINDERS

MONDAY

9:00 AM	4:00 PM
10:00 AM	5:00 PM
11:00 AM	6:00 PM
12:00 PM	MUST DOs
1:00 PM	☐
2:00 PM	☐
3:00 PM	☐

TUESDAY

9:00 AM	4:00 PM
10:00 AM	5:00 PM
11:00 AM	6:00 PM
12:00 PM	MUST DOs
1:00 PM	☐
2:00 PM	☐
3:00 PM	☐

WEDNESDAY

9:00 AM	4:00 PM
10:00 AM	5:00 PM
11:00 AM	6:00 PM
12:00 PM	MUST DOs
1:00 PM	☐
2:00 PM	☐
3:00 PM	☐

THURSDAY

9:00 AM	4:00 PM
10:00 AM	5:00 PM
11:00 AM	6:00 PM
12:00 PM	MUST DOs
1:00 PM	☐
2:00 PM	☐
3:00 PM	☐

FRIDAY

9:00 AM	4:00 PM
10:00 AM	5:00 PM
11:00 AM	6:00 PM
12:00 PM	MUST DOs
1:00 PM	☐
2:00 PM	☐
3:00 PM	☐

SATURDAY
APPOINTMENTS

SUNDAY
APPOINTMENTS

_____

_____

_____

MUST DOs

☐

☐

MUST DOs

☐

☐

NOTES

....

....

....

....

MONDAY

9:00 AM	4:00 PM
10:00 AM	5:00 PM
11:00 AM	6:00 PM
12:00 PM	MUST DOs
1:00 PM	☐
2:00 PM	☐
3:00 PM	☐

TUESDAY

9:00 AM	4:00 PM
10:00 AM	5:00 PM
11:00 AM	6:00 PM
12:00 PM	MUST DOs
1:00 PM	☐
2:00 PM	☐
3:00 PM	☐

WEDNESDAY

9:00 AM	4:00 PM
10:00 AM	5:00 PM
11:00 AM	6:00 PM
12:00 PM	MUST DOs
1:00 PM	☐
2:00 PM	☐
3:00 PM	☐

THURSDAY

9:00 AM	4:00 PM
10:00 AM	5:00 PM
11:00 AM	6:00 PM
12:00 PM	MUST DOs
1:00 PM	☐
2:00 PM	☐
3:00 PM	☐

FRIDAY

9:00 AM	4:00 PM
10:00 AM	5:00 PM
11:00 AM	6:00 PM
12:00 PM	MUST DOs
1:00 PM	☐
2:00 PM	☐
3:00 PM	☐

SATURDAY
APPOINTMENTS

SUNDAY
APPOINTMENTS

MUST DOs

☐

☐

MUST DOs

☐

☐

NOTES

PAYABLE TRACKER

DATE	BILL	AMOUNT

NOTES

EMAIL TRACKER

DATE	SUBJECT	FROM

REMINDERS

MONDAY

9:00 AM	4:00 PM
10:00 AM	5:00 PM
11:00 AM	6:00 PM
12:00 PM	MUST DOs
1:00 PM	☐
2:00 PM	☐
3:00 PM	☐

TUESDAY

9:00 AM	4:00 PM
10:00 AM	5:00 PM
11:00 AM	6:00 PM
12:00 PM	MUST DOs
1:00 PM	☐
2:00 PM	☐
3:00 PM	☐

WEDNESDAY

9:00 AM	4:00 PM
10:00 AM	5:00 PM
11:00 AM	6:00 PM
12:00 PM	MUST DOs
1:00 PM	☐
2:00 PM	☐
3:00 PM	☐

THURSDAY

9:00 AM	4:00 PM
10:00 AM	5:00 PM
11:00 AM	6:00 PM
12:00 PM	MUST DOs
1:00 PM	☐
2:00 PM	☐
3:00 PM	☐

FRIDAY

9:00 AM	4:00 PM
10:00 AM	5:00 PM
11:00 AM	6:00 PM
12:00 PM	MUST DOs
1:00 PM	☐
2:00 PM	☐
3:00 PM	☐

SATURDAY
APPOINTMENTS

SUNDAY
APPOINTMENTS

MUST DOs
☐
☐

MUST DOs
☐
☐

NOTES

....

....

....

....

MONDAY

9:00 AM	4:00 PM
10:00 AM	5:00 PM
11:00 AM	6:00 PM
12:00 PM	MUST DOs
1:00 PM	☐
2:00 PM	☐
3:00 PM	☐

TUESDAY

9:00 AM	4:00 PM
10:00 AM	5:00 PM
11:00 AM	6:00 PM
12:00 PM	MUST DOs
1:00 PM	☐
2:00 PM	☐
3:00 PM	☐

WEDNESDAY

9:00 AM	4:00 PM
10:00 AM	5:00 PM
11:00 AM	6:00 PM
12:00 PM	MUST DOs
1:00 PM	☐
2:00 PM	☐
3:00 PM	☐

THURSDAY

9:00 AM	4:00 PM
10:00 AM	5:00 PM
11:00 AM	6:00 PM
12:00 PM	MUST DOs
1:00 PM	☐
2:00 PM	☐
3:00 PM	☐

FRIDAY

9:00 AM	4:00 PM
10:00 AM	5:00 PM
11:00 AM	6:00 PM
12:00 PM	MUST DOs
1:00 PM	☐
2:00 PM	☐
3:00 PM	☐

SATURDAY
APPOINTMENTS

SUNDAY
APPOINTMENTS

MUST DOs

☐
☐

MUST DOs

☐
☐

NOTES

....

....

....

....

PAYABLE TRACKER <<<<<<<<

DATE	BILL	AMOUNT

>>>>>>>> NOTES

EMAIL TRACKER

DATE	SUBJECT	FROM

REMINDERS

MONDAY

9:00 AM	4:00 PM
10:00 AM	5:00 PM
11:00 AM	6:00 PM
12:00 PM	MUST DOs
1:00 PM	☐
2:00 PM	☐
3:00 PM	☐

TUESDAY

9:00 AM	4:00 PM
10:00 AM	5:00 PM
11:00 AM	6:00 PM
12:00 PM	MUST DOs
1:00 PM	☐
2:00 PM	☐
3:00 PM	☐

WEDNESDAY

9:00 AM	4:00 PM
10:00 AM	5:00 PM
11:00 AM	6:00 PM
12:00 PM	MUST DOs
1:00 PM	☐
2:00 PM	☐
3:00 PM	☐

THURSDAY

9:00 AM	4:00 PM
10:00 AM	5:00 PM
11:00 AM	6:00 PM
12:00 PM	MUST DOs
1:00 PM	☐
2:00 PM	☐
3:00 PM	☐

FRIDAY

9:00 AM	4:00 PM
10:00 AM	5:00 PM
11:00 AM	6:00 PM
12:00 PM	MUST DOs
1:00 PM	☐
2:00 PM	☐
3:00 PM	☐

SATURDAY
APPOINTMENTS

SUNDAY
APPOINTMENTS

MUST DOs

☐

☐

MUST DOs

☐

☐

NOTES

....

....

....

....

MONDAY

9:00 AM	4:00 PM
10:00 AM	5:00 PM
11:00 AM	6:00 PM
12:00 PM	MUST DOs
1:00 PM	☐
2:00 PM	☐
3:00 PM	☐

TUESDAY

9:00 AM	4:00 PM
10:00 AM	5:00 PM
11:00 AM	6:00 PM
12:00 PM	MUST DOs
1:00 PM	☐
2:00 PM	☐
3:00 PM	☐

WEDNESDAY

9:00 AM	4:00 PM
10:00 AM	5:00 PM
11:00 AM	6:00 PM
12:00 PM	MUST DOs
1:00 PM	☐
2:00 PM	☐
3:00 PM	☐

THURSDAY

9:00 AM	4:00 PM
10:00 AM	5:00 PM
11:00 AM	6:00 PM
12:00 PM	MUST DOs
1:00 PM	☐
2:00 PM	☐
3:00 PM	☐

FRIDAY

9:00 AM	4:00 PM
10:00 AM	5:00 PM
11:00 AM	6:00 PM
12:00 PM	MUST DOs
1:00 PM	☐
2:00 PM	☐
3:00 PM	☐

SATURDAY
APPOINTMENTS

_____

_____

_____

MUST DOs

☐ _____

☐ _____

SUNDAY
APPOINTMENTS

_____

_____

_____

MUST DOs

☐ _____

☐ _____

NOTES

....

....

....

....

PAYABLE TRACKER

DATE	BILL	AMOUNT

NOTES

_____

_____

_____

_____

_____

_____

_____

_____

_____

_____

EMAIL TRACKER

DATE	SUBJECT	FROM

REMINDERS

MONDAY

9:00 AM	4:00 PM
10:00 AM	5:00 PM
11:00 AM	6:00 PM
12:00 PM	MUST DOs
1:00 PM	☐
2:00 PM	☐
3:00 PM	☐

TUESDAY

9:00 AM	4:00 PM
10:00 AM	5:00 PM
11:00 AM	6:00 PM
12:00 PM	MUST DOs
1:00 PM	☐
2:00 PM	☐
3:00 PM	☐

WEDNESDAY

9:00 AM	4:00 PM
10:00 AM	5:00 PM
11:00 AM	6:00 PM
12:00 PM	MUST DOs
1:00 PM	☐
2:00 PM	☐
3:00 PM	☐

THURSDAY

9:00 AM	4:00 PM
10:00 AM	5:00 PM
11:00 AM	6:00 PM
12:00 PM	MUST DOs
1:00 PM	☐
2:00 PM	☐
3:00 PM	☐

FRIDAY

9:00 AM	4:00 PM
10:00 AM	5:00 PM
11:00 AM	6:00 PM
12:00 PM	MUST DOs
1:00 PM	☐
2:00 PM	☐
3:00 PM	☐

SATURDAY
APPOINTMENTS

SUNDAY
APPOINTMENTS

MUST DOs

☐
☐

MUST DOs

☐
☐

NOTES

....

....

....

....

MONDAY

9:00 AM	4:00 PM
10:00 AM	5:00 PM
11:00 AM	6:00 PM
12:00 PM	MUST DOs
1:00 PM	☐
2:00 PM	☐
3:00 PM	☐

TUESDAY

9:00 AM	4:00 PM
10:00 AM	5:00 PM
11:00 AM	6:00 PM
12:00 PM	MUST DOs
1:00 PM	☐
2:00 PM	☐
3:00 PM	☐

WEDNESDAY

9:00 AM	4:00 PM
10:00 AM	5:00 PM
11:00 AM	6:00 PM
12:00 PM	MUST DOs
1:00 PM	☐
2:00 PM	☐
3:00 PM	☐

THURSDAY

9:00 AM	4:00 PM
10:00 AM	5:00 PM
11:00 AM	6:00 PM
12:00 PM	MUST DOs
1:00 PM	☐
2:00 PM	☐
3:00 PM	☐

FRIDAY

9:00 AM	4:00 PM
10:00 AM	5:00 PM
11:00 AM	6:00 PM
12:00 PM	MUST DOs
1:00 PM	☐
2:00 PM	☐
3:00 PM	☐

SATURDAY
APPOINTMENTS

SUNDAY
APPOINTMENTS

_____

_____

_____

MUST DOs

☐

☐

MUST DOs

☐

☐

NOTES

....

....

....

....

PAYABLE TRACKER <<<<<<<<<<<<<

DATE	BILL	AMOUNT

>>>>>>>>>>>>> NOTES

EMAIL TRACKER

DATE	SUBJECT	FROM

REMINDERS

MONDAY

9:00 AM	4:00 PM
10:00 AM	5:00 PM
11:00 AM	6:00 PM
12:00 PM	MUST DOs
1:00 PM	☐
2:00 PM	☐
3:00 PM	☐

TUESDAY

9:00 AM	4:00 PM
10:00 AM	5:00 PM
11:00 AM	6:00 PM
12:00 PM	MUST DOs
1:00 PM	☐
2:00 PM	☐
3:00 PM	☐

WEDNESDAY

9:00 AM	4:00 PM
10:00 AM	5:00 PM
11:00 AM	6:00 PM
12:00 PM	MUST DOs
1:00 PM	☐
2:00 PM	☐
3:00 PM	☐

THURSDAY

9:00 AM	4:00 PM
10:00 AM	5:00 PM
11:00 AM	6:00 PM
12:00 PM	MUST DOs
1:00 PM	☐
2:00 PM	☐
3:00 PM	☐

FRIDAY

9:00 AM	4:00 PM
10:00 AM	5:00 PM
11:00 AM	6:00 PM
12:00 PM	MUST DOs
1:00 PM	☐
2:00 PM	☐
3:00 PM	☐

SATURDAY
APPOINTMENTS

_____

_____

MUST DOs
☐
☐

SUNDAY
APPOINTMENTS

_____

_____

MUST DOs
☐
☐

NOTES

....

....

....

....

MONDAY

9:00 AM	4:00 PM
10:00 AM	5:00 PM
11:00 AM	6:00 PM
12:00 PM	MUST DOs
1:00 PM	☐
2:00 PM	☐
3:00 PM	☐

TUESDAY

9:00 AM	4:00 PM
10:00 AM	5:00 PM
11:00 AM	6:00 PM
12:00 PM	MUST DOs
1:00 PM	☐
2:00 PM	☐
3:00 PM	☐

WEDNESDAY

9:00 AM	4:00 PM
10:00 AM	5:00 PM
11:00 AM	6:00 PM
12:00 PM	MUST DOs
1:00 PM	☐
2:00 PM	☐
3:00 PM	☐

THURSDAY

9:00 AM	4:00 PM
10:00 AM	5:00 PM
11:00 AM	6:00 PM
12:00 PM	MUST DOs
1:00 PM	☐
2:00 PM	☐
3:00 PM	☐

FRIDAY

9:00 AM	4:00 PM
10:00 AM	5:00 PM
11:00 AM	6:00 PM
12:00 PM	MUST DOs
1:00 PM	☐
2:00 PM	☐
3:00 PM	☐

SATURDAY
APPOINTMENTS

SUNDAY
APPOINTMENTS

MUST DOs

☐

☐

MUST DOs

☐

☐

NOTES

....

....

....

....

PAYABLE TRACKER

DATE	BILL	AMOUNT

NOTES

EMAIL TRACKER

DATE	SUBJECT	FROM

REMINDERS

MONDAY

9:00 AM	4:00 PM
10:00 AM	5:00 PM
11:00 AM	6:00 PM
12:00 PM	MUST DOs
1:00 PM	☐
2:00 PM	☐
3:00 PM	☐

TUESDAY

9:00 AM	4:00 PM
10:00 AM	5:00 PM
11:00 AM	6:00 PM
12:00 PM	MUST DOs
1:00 PM	☐
2:00 PM	☐
3:00 PM	☐

WEDNESDAY

9:00 AM	4:00 PM
10:00 AM	5:00 PM
11:00 AM	6:00 PM
12:00 PM	MUST DOs
1:00 PM	☐
2:00 PM	☐
3:00 PM	☐

THURSDAY

9:00 AM	4:00 PM
10:00 AM	5:00 PM
11:00 AM	6:00 PM
12:00 PM	MUST DOs
1:00 PM	☐
2:00 PM	☐
3:00 PM	☐

FRIDAY

9:00 AM	4:00 PM
10:00 AM	5:00 PM
11:00 AM	6:00 PM
12:00 PM	MUST DOs
1:00 PM	☐
2:00 PM	☐
3:00 PM	☐

SATURDAY
APPOINTMENTS

SUNDAY
APPOINTMENTS

MUST DOs
☐
☐

MUST DOs
☐
☐

NOTES

....

....

....

....

MONDAY

9:00 AM	4:00 PM
10:00 AM	5:00 PM
11:00 AM	6:00 PM
12:00 PM	MUST DOs
1:00 PM	☐
2:00 PM	☐
3:00 PM	☐

TUESDAY

9:00 AM	4:00 PM
10:00 AM	5:00 PM
11:00 AM	6:00 PM
12:00 PM	MUST DOs
1:00 PM	☐
2:00 PM	☐
3:00 PM	☐

WEDNESDAY

9:00 AM	4:00 PM
10:00 AM	5:00 PM
11:00 AM	6:00 PM
12:00 PM	MUST DOs
1:00 PM	☐
2:00 PM	☐
3:00 PM	☐

THURSDAY

9:00 AM	4:00 PM
10:00 AM	5:00 PM
11:00 AM	6:00 PM
12:00 PM	MUST DOs
1:00 PM	☐
2:00 PM	☐
3:00 PM	☐

FRIDAY

9:00 AM	4:00 PM
10:00 AM	5:00 PM
11:00 AM	6:00 PM
12:00 PM	MUST DOs
1:00 PM	☐
2:00 PM	☐
3:00 PM	☐

SATURDAY
APPOINTMENTS

SUNDAY
APPOINTMENTS

MUST DOs
☐
☐

MUST DOs
☐
☐

NOTES

....

....

....

....

PAYABLE TRACKER

DATE	BILL	AMOUNT

NOTES

EMAIL TRACKER

DATE	SUBJECT	FROM

REMINDERS

MONDAY

9:00 AM	4:00 PM
10:00 AM	5:00 PM
11:00 AM	6:00 PM
12:00 PM	MUST DOs
1:00 PM	☐
2:00 PM	☐
3:00 PM	☐

TUESDAY

9:00 AM	4:00 PM
10:00 AM	5:00 PM
11:00 AM	6:00 PM
12:00 PM	MUST DOs
1:00 PM	☐
2:00 PM	☐
3:00 PM	☐

WEDNESDAY

9:00 AM	4:00 PM
10:00 AM	5:00 PM
11:00 AM	6:00 PM
12:00 PM	MUST DOs
1:00 PM	☐
2:00 PM	☐
3:00 PM	☐

THURSDAY

9:00 AM	4:00 PM
10:00 AM	5:00 PM
11:00 AM	6:00 PM
12:00 PM	MUST DOs
1:00 PM	☐
2:00 PM	☐
3:00 PM	☐

FRIDAY

9:00 AM	4:00 PM
10:00 AM	5:00 PM
11:00 AM	6:00 PM
12:00 PM	MUST DOs
1:00 PM	☐
2:00 PM	☐
3:00 PM	☐

SATURDAY
APPOINTMENTS

SUNDAY
APPOINTMENTS

MUST DOs

☐

☐

MUST DOs

☐

☐

NOTES

....

....

....

....

MONDAY

9:00 AM	4:00 PM
10:00 AM	5:00 PM
11:00 AM	6:00 PM
12:00 PM	MUST DOs
1:00 PM	☐
2:00 PM	☐
3:00 PM	☐

TUESDAY

9:00 AM	4:00 PM
10:00 AM	5:00 PM
11:00 AM	6:00 PM
12:00 PM	MUST DOs
1:00 PM	☐
2:00 PM	☐
3:00 PM	☐

WEDNESDAY

9:00 AM	4:00 PM
10:00 AM	5:00 PM
11:00 AM	6:00 PM
12:00 PM	MUST DOs
1:00 PM	☐
2:00 PM	☐
3:00 PM	☐

THURSDAY

9:00 AM	4:00 PM
10:00 AM	5:00 PM
11:00 AM	6:00 PM
12:00 PM	MUST DOs
1:00 PM	☐
2:00 PM	☐
3:00 PM	☐

FRIDAY

9:00 AM	4:00 PM
10:00 AM	5:00 PM
11:00 AM	6:00 PM
12:00 PM	MUST DOs
1:00 PM	☐
2:00 PM	☐
3:00 PM	☐

SATURDAY
APPOINTMENTS

SUNDAY
APPOINTMENTS

MUST DOs

☐
☐

MUST DOs

☐
☐

NOTES

PAYABLE TRACKER 《《《《《《《《《

DATE	BILL	AMOUNT

》》》》》》》》》 NOTES

EMAIL TRACKER

DATE	SUBJECT	FROM

REMINDERS

MONDAY

9:00 AM	4:00 PM
10:00 AM	5:00 PM
11:00 AM	6:00 PM
12:00 PM	MUST DOs
1:00 PM	☐
2:00 PM	☐
3:00 PM	☐

TUESDAY

9:00 AM	4:00 PM
10:00 AM	5:00 PM
11:00 AM	6:00 PM
12:00 PM	MUST DOs
1:00 PM	☐
2:00 PM	☐
3:00 PM	☐

WEDNESDAY

9:00 AM	4:00 PM
10:00 AM	5:00 PM
11:00 AM	6:00 PM
12:00 PM	MUST DOs
1:00 PM	☐
2:00 PM	☐
3:00 PM	☐

THURSDAY

9:00 AM	4:00 PM
10:00 AM	5:00 PM
11:00 AM	6:00 PM
12:00 PM	MUST DOs
1:00 PM	☐
2:00 PM	☐
3:00 PM	☐

FRIDAY

9:00 AM	4:00 PM
10:00 AM	5:00 PM
11:00 AM	6:00 PM
12:00 PM	MUST DOs
1:00 PM	☐
2:00 PM	☐
3:00 PM	☐

SATURDAY
APPOINTMENTS

SUNDAY
APPOINTMENTS

MUST DOs
☐
☐

MUST DOs
☐
☐

NOTES

MONDAY

9:00 AM	4:00 PM
10:00 AM	5:00 PM
11:00 AM	6:00 PM
12:00 PM	MUST DOs
1:00 PM	☐
2:00 PM	☐
3:00 PM	☐

TUESDAY

9:00 AM	4:00 PM
10:00 AM	5:00 PM
11:00 AM	6:00 PM
12:00 PM	MUST DOs
1:00 PM	☐
2:00 PM	☐
3:00 PM	☐

WEDNESDAY

9:00 AM	4:00 PM
10:00 AM	5:00 PM
11:00 AM	6:00 PM
12:00 PM	MUST DOs
1:00 PM	☐
2:00 PM	☐
3:00 PM	☐

THURSDAY

9:00 AM	4:00 PM
10:00 AM	5:00 PM
11:00 AM	6:00 PM
12:00 PM	MUST DOs
1:00 PM	☐
2:00 PM	☐
3:00 PM	☐

FRIDAY

9:00 AM	4:00 PM
10:00 AM	5:00 PM
11:00 AM	6:00 PM
12:00 PM	MUST DOs
1:00 PM	☐
2:00 PM	☐
3:00 PM	☐

SATURDAY
APPOINTMENTS

SUNDAY
APPOINTMENTS

MUST DOs
☐
☐

MUST DOs
☐
☐

NOTES

....

....

....

....

PAYABLE TRACKER ⫸

DATE	BILL	AMOUNT

⫸ NOTES

EMAIL TRACKER

DATE	SUBJECT	FROM

REMINDERS

MONDAY

9:00 AM	4:00 PM
10:00 AM	5:00 PM
11:00 AM	6:00 PM
12:00 PM	MUST DOs
1:00 PM	☐
2:00 PM	☐
3:00 PM	☐

TUESDAY

9:00 AM	4:00 PM
10:00 AM	5:00 PM
11:00 AM	6:00 PM
12:00 PM	MUST DOs
1:00 PM	☐
2:00 PM	☐
3:00 PM	☐

WEDNESDAY

9:00 AM	4:00 PM
10:00 AM	5:00 PM
11:00 AM	6:00 PM
12:00 PM	MUST DOs
1:00 PM	☐
2:00 PM	☐
3:00 PM	☐

THURSDAY

9:00 AM	4:00 PM
10:00 AM	5:00 PM
11:00 AM	6:00 PM
12:00 PM	MUST DOs
1:00 PM	☐
2:00 PM	☐
3:00 PM	☐

FRIDAY

9:00 AM	4:00 PM
10:00 AM	5:00 PM
11:00 AM	6:00 PM
12:00 PM	MUST DOs
1:00 PM	☐
2:00 PM	☐
3:00 PM	☐

SATURDAY
APPOINTMENTS

SUNDAY
APPOINTMENTS

MUST DOs
☐
☐

MUST DOs
☐
☐

NOTES

....

....

....

....

MONDAY

9:00 AM	4:00 PM
10:00 AM	5:00 PM
11:00 AM	6:00 PM
12:00 PM	MUST DOs
1:00 PM	☐
2:00 PM	☐
3:00 PM	☐

TUESDAY

9:00 AM	4:00 PM
10:00 AM	5:00 PM
11:00 AM	6:00 PM
12:00 PM	MUST DOs
1:00 PM	☐
2:00 PM	☐
3:00 PM	☐

WEDNESDAY

9:00 AM	4:00 PM
10:00 AM	5:00 PM
11:00 AM	6:00 PM
12:00 PM	MUST DOs
1:00 PM	☐
2:00 PM	☐
3:00 PM	☐

THURSDAY

9:00 AM	4:00 PM
10:00 AM	5:00 PM
11:00 AM	6:00 PM
12:00 PM	MUST DOs
1:00 PM	☐
2:00 PM	☐
3:00 PM	☐

FRIDAY

9:00 AM	4:00 PM
10:00 AM	5:00 PM
11:00 AM	6:00 PM
12:00 PM	MUST DOs
1:00 PM	☐
2:00 PM	☐
3:00 PM	☐

SATURDAY
APPOINTMENTS

SUNDAY
APPOINTMENTS

MUST DOs

☐

☐

MUST DOs

☐

☐

NOTES

PAYABLE TRACKER

DATE	BILL	AMOUNT

NOTES

_____
_____
_____
_____
_____
_____
_____
_____

EMAIL TRACKER

DATE	SUBJECT	FROM

REMINDERS

MONDAY

9:00 AM	4:00 PM
10:00 AM	5:00 PM
11:00 AM	6:00 PM
12:00 PM	MUST DOs
1:00 PM	☐
2:00 PM	☐
3:00 PM	☐

TUESDAY

9:00 AM	4:00 PM
10:00 AM	5:00 PM
11:00 AM	6:00 PM
12:00 PM	MUST DOs
1:00 PM	☐
2:00 PM	☐
3:00 PM	☐

WEDNESDAY

9:00 AM	4:00 PM
10:00 AM	5:00 PM
11:00 AM	6:00 PM
12:00 PM	MUST DOs
1:00 PM	☐
2:00 PM	☐
3:00 PM	☐

THURSDAY

9:00 AM	4:00 PM
10:00 AM	5:00 PM
11:00 AM	6:00 PM
12:00 PM	MUST DOs
1:00 PM	☐
2:00 PM	☐
3:00 PM	☐

FRIDAY

9:00 AM	4:00 PM
10:00 AM	5:00 PM
11:00 AM	6:00 PM
12:00 PM	MUST DOs
1:00 PM	☐
2:00 PM	☐
3:00 PM	☐

SATURDAY
APPOINTMENTS

SUNDAY
APPOINTMENTS

MUST DOs

☐

☐

MUST DOs

☐

☐

NOTES

....

....

....

....

MONDAY

9:00 AM	4:00 PM
10:00 AM	5:00 PM
11:00 AM	6:00 PM
12:00 PM	MUST DOs
1:00 PM	☐
2:00 PM	☐
3:00 PM	☐

TUESDAY

9:00 AM	4:00 PM
10:00 AM	5:00 PM
11:00 AM	6:00 PM
12:00 PM	MUST DOs
1:00 PM	☐
2:00 PM	☐
3:00 PM	☐

WEDNESDAY

9:00 AM	4:00 PM
10:00 AM	5:00 PM
11:00 AM	6:00 PM
12:00 PM	MUST DOs
1:00 PM	☐
2:00 PM	☐
3:00 PM	☐

THURSDAY

9:00 AM	4:00 PM
10:00 AM	5:00 PM
11:00 AM	6:00 PM
12:00 PM	MUST DOs
1:00 PM	☐
2:00 PM	☐
3:00 PM	☐

FRIDAY

9:00 AM	4:00 PM
10:00 AM	5:00 PM
11:00 AM	6:00 PM
12:00 PM	MUST DOs
1:00 PM	☐
2:00 PM	☐
3:00 PM	☐

SATURDAY
APPOINTMENTS

SUNDAY
APPOINTMENTS

MUST DOs

☐
☐

MUST DOs

☐
☐

NOTES

....

....

....

....

PAYABLE TRACKER <<<<<<<<<<<<<

DATE	BILL	AMOUNT

>>>>>>>>>>>> NOTES

_____
_____
_____
_____
_____
_____
_____
_____

EMAIL TRACKER

DATE	SUBJECT	FROM

REMINDERS

www.ingramcontent.com/pod-product-compliance
Lightning Source LLC
Chambersburg PA
CBHW081338090426
42737CB00017B/3198